RECORD BREAKERS

RECORD-BREAKING BUILDINGS

DANIEL GILPIN

PowerKiDS press™

New York

Published in 2012 by The Rosen Publishing Group Inc.
29 East 21st Street, New York, NY 10010

First Edition

Senior Editor: Debbie Foy
Designer: Rob Walster
Picture Researcher: Kate Lockley

Library of Congress Cataloging-in-Publication Data

Gilpin, Daniel.
Record-breaking buildings / by Daniel Gilpin. -- 1st ed.
    p. cm. -- (Record breakers)
Includes index.
ISBN 978-1-4488-5288-8 (library binding)
1. Buildings--Juvenile literature. 2. World records--Juvenile
literature. I. Title.
TH149.G55 2012
720--dc22

                    2010047269

Manufactured in China
CPSIA Compliance Information: Batch #WAS1102PK: For Further Information
contact Rosen Publishing, New York, New York at 1-800-237-9932

Photographs:

Alessandra Benedetti/Corbis: 22T
Peter Bowater/Alamy: 12–13
Brunei Information Department/Reuters/
    Corbis: 20–21
Joseph Calev/Shutterstock: 19
Dominique Debaralle/Sygma/Corbis: 16 (inset)
Reinhard Dirscherl/Alamy: 26
Jeremy Edwards/iStockphoto: 2, 10
Stephen Ferry/Liaison/Getty Images: 4–5
Colin Galloway/Alamy: 13 (inset)
Mike Goldwater/Alamy: 14
Mark Hamilton/Alamy: COVER, 24(inset)
Lizzie Himmel/Sygma/Corbis: 4(inset)
Mick Hutson/Redferns/Getty Images: 24–25
Ingo Jezierski/Corbis: 20(inset)
KPA/Zuma/Rex Features: 8(inset)
Jean-Pierre Lescourret/Corbis: 18–19
Kees Metselaar/Alamy: 6–7
© Johan Möller: 23
Ralf Noehmer/iStockphoto: 28, 30
Kiyoshi Ota/Getty Images: 29
Louie Psihoyos/Corbis: 8–9
© Screen Room Cinema: 22B
Sculpies/Shutterstock: 26–27
Tyler Stalman/iStockphoto: 10–11
Stringer/Korea/Reuters/Corbis: 16–17
Sandro Vannini/Corbis: 15
Evan Wong/Shutterstock: 6

Abbreviations used:

ft. = feet
m = meters
km = kilometers
cu. ft. = cubic feet
cu. m = cubic meters
sq. mi. = square miles
sq. km = square kilometers
sq. ft. = square feet
sq. m = square meters

Tricky words are listed in "But What
Does That Mean?" on page 31.

WHAT'S INSIDE?

ADX FLORENCE

ADX Florence is the world's most secure prison. Located deep in the wild Rocky Mountains south of Florence, Colorado, it is known as the "Alcatraz of the Rockies."

MOST SECURE PRISON!

Can You Believe It?

ADX Florence houses some of the most dangerous criminals in the U.S. Its inmates are nearly all serial killers, terrorists, gang bosses, or drug lords.

UP CLOSE

A typical cell at ADX Florence has furniture made from concrete and a thin strip of window!

The area between the inner prison fence and the razor-wire fence is crossed with laser beam sensors and guarded by attack dogs!

The prison is surrounded by armed guards who sit in tall watchtowers overlooking the prison grounds!

WOW!

THE PRISON IS SURROUNDED BY A 12 FT. (3.6 M) RAZOR-WIRE FENCE. MOST OF THE INMATES ARE KEPT IN SOLITARY CONFINEMENT FOR AT LEAST 23 HOURS A DAY.

ANGKOR WAT

Angkor Wat in Cambodia is the world's largest religious structure. Now a ruin, it was built by a king in the twelfth century to honor a Hindu god.

Can You Believe It?

Angkor Wat was home to around 80,000 people! Many of these people were priests or servants of the king.

UP CLOSE

Angkor Wat fell into ruin in the sixteenth century and became overgrown by the surrounding jungle. Today, the jungle has been cleared from part of the Wat, but other areas are still covered by twisty roots.

WOW!

ANGKOR WAT COVERS AN AREA OF 0.6 SQ. MI. (1.6 SQ. KM). THIS IS 377 TIMES THE AREA OF THE WHITE HOUSE IN WASHINGTON, DC.

Over 2 million tourists visit Angkor Wat every year.

BOEING EVERETT FACTORY

BIGGEST BUILDING!

The Boeing Everett factory is the biggest building on Earth. Located near Seattle, Washington, the factory is used by Boeing to construct its aircraft.

Can You Believe It?

The factory operates around the clock, with around 10,000 workers in the building at any one time! Boeing also runs tours of the factory, showing 180,000 visitors around each year.

A brand new Boeing 787 outside the factory attracts a large crowd.

Three Boeing 747s, or jumbo jets, stand side by side on the enormous factory floor!

WOW!

THE BOEING FACTORY HAS A TOTAL VOLUME OF 472 MILLION CU. FT. (13.3 MILLION CU. M). THIS IS 135 TIMES THE SIZE OF LONDON'S ROYAL ALBERT HALL!

CONTENDERS

Although the Boeing Everett factory has a bigger volume, Terminal 3 of Dubai International airport has a larger floor area. It is more than 200 times the size of a football field!

GRAND CENTRAL TERMINAL

New York's Grand Central Terminal is the world's biggest railroad station. More than half a million people pass through Grand Central Station every day!

Can You Believe It?

Located in Manhattan, New York, the station serves 660 commuter trains, carrying workers to and from New York City.

The busy drop-off area of Grand Central Station.

Grand Central's main concourse is a popular meeting place for New Yorkers and visitors!

WOW!

THE STATION HAS 44 PLATFORMS AND 67 TRACKS, ALL BELOW GROUND AND ARRANGED OVER TWO LEVELS.

BURJ KHALIFA

WOW!

THE BURJ KHALIFA HAS 164 FLOORS AND STANDS AT A HEIGHT OF 2,684 FT. (818 M). IT ALSO HOLDS THE RECORD FOR THE LONGEST ELEVATOR IN THE WORLD!

The Burj Khalifa is the world's tallest building. The tip of its spire is more than 0.5 miles (0.8 km) above the ground!

Can You Believe It?

Standing almost twice as high as New York's Empire State Building, Dubai's Burj Khalifa officially opened in 2010 and cost an amazing $1.5 billion!

The Burj Khalifa took more than five years to build!

The Burj Khalifa took the world record from a building called the Taipei 101 in Taiwan.

CONTENDERS

In Kuwait, there are plans to build an even taller tower than the Burj Khalifa! It will be 3,284 ft. (1,001 m) tall and will take 25 years to build!

ICE HOTEL

The Ice Hotel in Jukkasjärvi, Sweden, is the world's largest building made of ice.

Can You Believe It?

The Ice Hotel melts in the spring and is rebuilt every fall, each time larger than before. Guests sleep in thick sleeping bags on beds made of ice!

The Ice Hotel is built from blocks of ice cut from a frozen river. This is the hotel's icy reception area!

14

DJENNE GRAND MOSQUE

Djenne Grand Mosque in Mali, Africa, is the world's largest building made from mud!

Can You Believe It?

The mosque was built in 1905 using millions of mud bricks. Most of the buildings in the surrounding town of Djenne were also built from mud!

LARGEST MUD BUILDING!

WOW!

DJENNE IS NEAR THE SAHARA DESERT AND GETS VERY LITTLE RAIN. BUT EACH YEAR, THE MOSQUE IS COVERED WITH A NEW LAYER OF MUD TO PROTECT IT FROM THE WEATHER.

MAY DAY STADIUM

BIGGEST STADIUM!

The Rungrado May Day is the world's biggest stadium. It is in Pyongyang, the capital of North Korea, and was built in 1989.

Can You Believe It?

The stadium hosts North Korea's Mass Games. Many thousands of athletes work together to create stunning performances. In 2002, one mass performance involved more than 100,000 people. This was a world record in its own right!

The May Day Stadium sits on a river island. The roof of its stands has 16 arches arranged in a circle.

CONTENDERS

Although it is not as big as the May Day Stadium, Brazil's Maracan Stadium has held more people. In 1950, 199,854 people attended soccer's World Cup Final there!

Thousands of people take part in a performance at the Mass Games held at the stadium.

WOW!

THE STADIUM CAN SEAT 150,000 PEOPLE AND HAS A TOTAL FLOOR AREA OF 2.2 MILLION SQ. FT. (210,000 SQ. M). ITS SEATING STANDS ARE EIGHT STORIES HIGH!

A huge $180 million was invested in the Rose Tower!

ROSE TOWER

Rose Tower in Dubai is the world's tallest hotel. Opening on December 22, 2009, this enormous building is 72 stories high!

Can You Believe It?

Rose Tower is only a few miles from the Burj Khalifa, the world's tallest building. Today, Dubai is one of the world's fastest (and tallest!) growing cities.

CONTENDERS

The Ryugyong Hotel in North Korea is still being built. But when it is finally finished, it may take over the title of the world's tallest hotel!

WOW!

ROSE TOWER IS 1,093 FT. (333 M) HIGH. IT HAS 482 ROOMS, SUITES, AND PENTHOUSES!

The Burj Al Arab used to be the tallest hotel in the world. It is shaped like a sail and sits on a man-made island in the sea!

ISTANA NURUL IMAN

Istana Nurul Iman in Borneo, Southeast Asia, is the biggest palace on Earth. It is the home of the Sultan of Brunei, one of the world's richest men.

Can You Believe It?

The Sultan of Brunei is said to own more than 3,000 cars, including 500 Rolls Royces. He also has his own private Boeing 747 jet, which is furnished with gold!

Istana Nurul Iman is built on the leafy banks of the Brunei River.

The Sultan has a vast collection of gold objects scattered through his palace. Even the toilet brush handles are gold-plated!

Important guests sit in the palace's throne hall.

WOW!

THE PALACE COVERS AN AREA OF OVER 2 MILLION SQ. FT. (200,000 SQ. M). IT HAS 1,788 ROOMS, INCLUDING 257 BATHROOMS!

SCREEN ROOM

The Screen Room in Nottingham, UK, is the world's smallest public movie theater. It has just one screen and a total of 21 seats!

Can You Believe It?

The Screen Room is such a small business that payment for tickets is by cash or check only.

Customers enjoy a movie at the Screen Room.

The plush seats are a comfortable experience for just 21 customers!

CROSS ISLAND CHAPEL

Cross Island Chapel is the world's smallest church. It sits on a tiny platform in the middle of a lake in the town of Oneida, New York.

Can You Believe It?

Cross Island Chapel only has room for three people to stand up inside. In 1990, a couple was married there. The rest of the wedding party had to sit in boats on the lake outside!

SMALLEST CHURCH!

On the Other Hand...

St. Peter's Basilica in Vatican City, Rome, is the world's largest church. It can hold up to 60,000 people!

Welcome to Oneida, N.Y. - Home of
CROSS ISLAND CHAPEL
BUILT IN 1989
THE WORLDS SMALLEST CHURCH →
Floor Area 51" x 81"(28.68 sq.ft.) Seats 2 People
Non-Denominational and Open to the Public upon request
315-363-4488
Available for Special Occasions and Meditation
"Cross Island Chapel" is dedicated as a witness to God

THE O2

London's O2 is the world's largest dome. Built in 1999 to celebrate the new millennium, it was originally called the Millennium Dome. In 2005, it was renamed the O2, and today it hosts large concerts, exhibitions, and other events.

Can You Believe It?

The O2 has an indoor arena, a music club, a theater, exhibition space, and many bars and restaurants.

The O2 is a striking landmark. It has 12 yellow support towers, one for each month of the year!

Many big name musicians have played the O2, including Britney Spears, Kanye West, and Madonna.

The O2 arena can also be used as a sports venue and is set to host gymnastics and basketball in the 2012 Olympic Games.

WOW!

THE O2 DOME HAS AN OVERALL DIAMETER OF 1,181 FT. (365 M). ITS ARENA CAN SEAT OVER 20,000 PEOPLE!

GREAT PYRAMID OF GIZA

Close to Cairo, Egypt, is the site of the Great Pyramid of Giza—the world's tallest pyramid!

Can You Believe It?

The pyramid was built 4,500 years ago. It held the record for the world's tallest building for 3,800 years!

The pyramid was built from huge stone blocks.

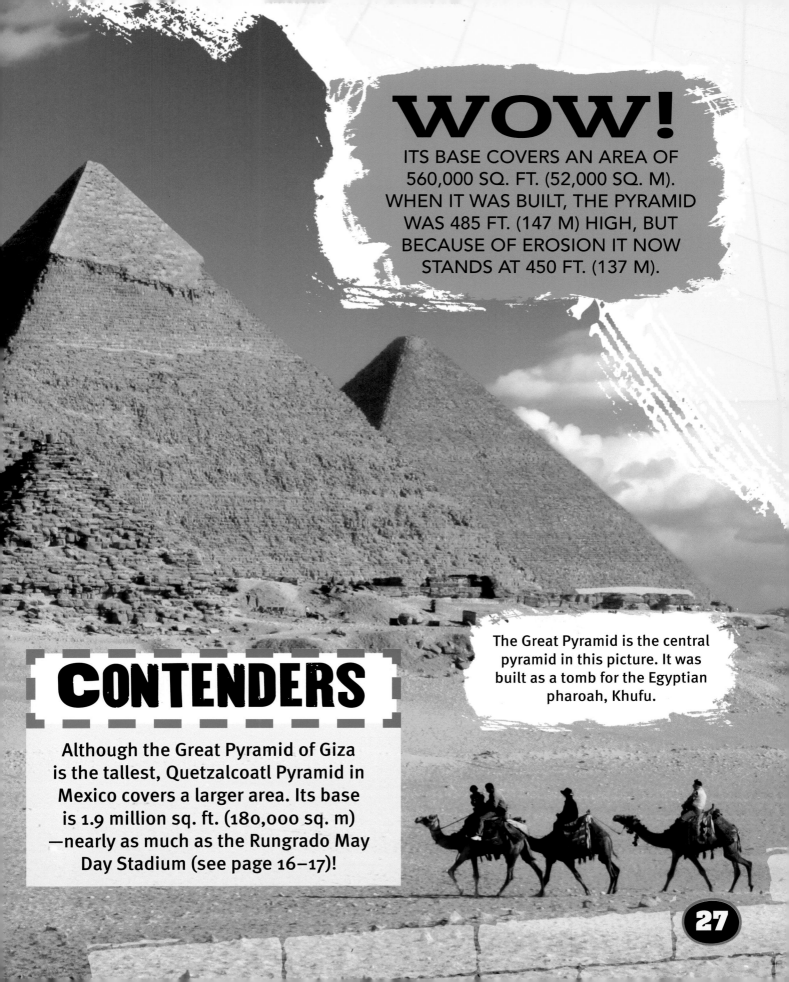

WOW!

ITS BASE COVERS AN AREA OF 560,000 SQ. FT. (52,000 SQ. M). WHEN IT WAS BUILT, THE PYRAMID WAS 485 FT. (147 M) HIGH, BUT BECAUSE OF EROSION IT NOW STANDS AT 450 FT. (137 M).

The Great Pyramid is the central pyramid in this picture. It was built as a tomb for the Egyptian pharoah, Khufu.

CONTENDERS

Although the Great Pyramid of Giza is the tallest, Quetzalcoatl Pyramid in Mexico covers a larger area. Its base is 1.9 million sq. ft. (180,000 sq. m) —nearly as much as the Rungrado May Day Stadium (see page 16–17)!

SUURHUSEN CHURCH

You may be surprised to hear that the world's most leaning building is in Germany. The steeple of Suurhusen Church leans at a truly amazing angle!

Can You Believe It?

When the church was built in 1450, its steeple was vertical. Over time, its wooden foundations have rotted, causing it to lean.

The church's steeple tilts at an angle of 5.19 degrees—a steeper angle than the Leaning Tower of Pisa!

YOKOHAMA MARINE TOWER

Yokohama Marine Tower was built in 1961, and sits overlooking the harbor in Yokohama, Japan.

Can You Believe It?

On a clear day, from the top of the tower, you can see the dormant volcano, Mount Fuji, 236 miles (380 km) away!

WOW!

THE LIGHTHOUSE STANDS AT 348 FT. (106 M) HIGH. DINERS IN THE TOWER-TOP RESTAURANT HAVE A STUNNING VIEW OVER YOKOHAMA BAY.

TEST YOURSELF!

Can you remember facts about the record-breaking buildings in this book? Test yourself here by answering these questions!

1. Which city has both the world's tallest building and the world's tallest hotel?
2. In which country is the world's largest religious structure?
3. True or false: The world's smallest church is in Italy?
4. Which aircraft company owns and uses the world's biggest building?
5. How many platforms does New York's Grand Central Terminal have?
6. In which city is the world's smallest public movie theater?
7. True or false: The world's most leaning building is the Leaning Tower of Pisa?
8. In which country is the world's largest ice building?
9. Since it was built, how much height has the Great Pyramid of Giza lost due to erosion?
10. In which country is the Djenne Grand Mosque?

Answers
1. Dubai
2. Cambodia
3. False, it is in the United States.
4. Boeing
5. 44
6. Nottingham, UK
7. False, it is Suurhusen Church, Germany
8. Sweden
9. 35 ft. (10 m)
10. Mali

BUT WHAT DOES THAT MEAN?

Alcatraz   This is a famously secure prison in San Francisco Bay, California.

arena   A large, enclosed area where concerts or sports events take place.

commuter   A person who travels from home to work, often by car, bus, or train.

diameter   The distance from one side of a circle to the other.

dormant   Sleeping or inactive.

erosion   The wearing away of stone or soil, often caused by water or wind.

foundations   Material placed below ground level to form the surface on which a building is built.

gold-plated   A thin layer of gold laid over another metal.

inmate   Another word for "prisoner."

mass performance   An organized performance often involving thousands of people.

millennium   A span of 1,000 years. The year 2000 was the beginning of the third millennium.

mosque   An Islamic religious building.

penthouse   An apartment located on the top floor (or floors) of a building.

plush   A thick, soft material.

razor-wire   Wire with sharp cutting edges, used on top of fences for security.

sensor   A device that can detect movement.

solitary confinement   When a prisoner is isolated from all other prisoners. It is often used as extra punishment for bad behavior.

spire   A pointed structure on top of a tower or steeple

steeple   A tall, pointed tower on a building, such as a church.

story   Another word for floor. An eight-story building has eight floors.

suite   In a hotel, this is a series of connected rooms that guests stay in.

vertical   Upright or pointing straight upward.

volume   The amount of space occupied by an area such as a room or building.

FURTHER INFORMATION, WEB SITES, AND INDEX

Places to go

Guinness World of Records
This amazing museum in Hollywood, California, has lots of great exhibits and information about record-breaking buildings.

Ripley's Believe It Or Not!
Ripley's attractions are packed with facts about record breakers. There are more than 70 of them in cities around the world.

Grand Central Terminal, New York
The world's biggest train station offers two free guided tours per week. Learn about the history and building of this famous landmark.

Books to read

Guinness World Records, 2011
(Guinness World Records, 2010)

Tallest Buildings and Structures in the World
by Frederic P. Miller (Alphascript Publishing, 2010)

Web Sites

Due to the changing nature of Internet links, PowerKids Press has developed an online list of Web sites related to the subject of this book. This site is updated regularly. Please use this link to access this list:
http://www.powerkidslinks.com/record/building/

Index